Original title:
The Cactus Chronicles

Copyright © 2025 Creative Arts Management OÜ
All rights reserved.

Author: Colin Harrington
ISBN HARDBACK: 978-1-80581-917-2
ISBN PAPERBACK: 978-1-80581-444-3
ISBN EBOOK: 978-1-80581-917-2

A Symphony of Spines

In the desert, spines all around,
They tickle my feet, no shoes can be found.
Each step I take causes a squeal,
A prickly concert, oh what a deal!

With a hat on my head and glee in my heart,
These prickly friends play a wild part.
A melody soon fills the hot air,
As I jiggle and dance with a cactus flair!

Echoes in the Dunes

Whispers of sand, they carry the tune,
As I tumble and roll, a clumsy cartoon.
"Watch out for spines!" my pals all shout,
But they're laughing too hard; what a goofy rout!

The dunes echo back with a chuckle and cheer,
Each tumble I take just adds to the fear.
Oh, cactus, my friend, so rugged and bold,
In this sandy ballet, our stories unfold!

Sunburnt Dreams

Under the sun, with dreams in my head,
I may look like a lobster, so bright and so red.
The cacti just grin, with their cool, calming vibes,
While I fan my sunburn, oh how it jibes!

I sip on a drink, with ice clinking loud,
And laugh at my pals, who say I'm too proud.
Yet my prickly pals stand tall and so grand,
In this sunny adventure, we frolic on sand!

Blooming in the Dry

In a land so parched, where troubles arise,
Cacti bloom bright, under wide-open skies.
Their flowers are goofy, with colors so bold,
Each petal a story, a secret retold!

As the sun shines down, they sway in the breeze,
While I try to dance, but stumble on these.
The blooms giggle softly, in their cactus delight,
"Come join us, my friend, in this hot, funny fight!"

Mirage in Bloom

In a desert so dry, where the sun likes to bake,
A cactus stands tall, no need for a break.
With arms in the air, it waves to the sky,
Saying, "Catch me a breeze or at least a butterfly!"

It wears all its spines like a prickly crown,
A king of the dunes, it won't let you frown.
When raindrops appear, oh what a big fuss,
Dancing and shouting, saying, "Join the circus!"

Guardians of the Arid Land

In the land that is sparse, our heroes stand tall,
Guardians of green, with no worries at all.
They soak up the sun and drink from the air,
With no fear of drought, they're beyond all compare!

A sage and a prickly, quite the odd pair,
Trading old stories while birds spin and dare.
"What's better than this?" asks the wise prickly friend,
"Dangers of water, that's a trend we'll defend!"

The Resilient Blooms

Oh, blooming with grit in this sandy expanse,
These plants throw a party, so come join the dance!
With petals like laughter and spines that protect,
They flourish in chaos, what did you expect?

In a world full of thorns, they giggle and grin,
Wearing nature's costume, they're all out to win.
So come take a seat, under shade on the floor,
Listen to tales of the blooms we adore!

Beneath the Sun's Gaze

Beneath the sun's gaze, our spiky friends thrive,
In a place where the heat makes the silly grass dive.
With laughter and colors that pop in the heat,
These green little jokers can't be beat!

They bask in the daylight, they're never quite shy,
Saying, "Look at us bloom, we're the stars of the sky!"
With humor and charm, they wiggle and sway,
In a world so parched, they're the life of the play!

Tales Beneath the Stars

In the quiet night, a cactus stood,
Telling tales of nights misunderstood.
With laughter and quirks, it shared its fate,
How it dodged a gardener's clumsy gait.

A tumbleweed rolled by to join the fun,
Whispering secrets beneath the moon's run.
They giggled at owls, all wise and aloof,
As the sand danced lightly, a soft, warm hoof.

Nomads roamed close, with jokes in their pack,
Their laughter erupted, like stars on the black.
Amongst these spines, a friendship took flight,
Under the vast and soft blanket of night.

The Desert's Gentle Heart

In the sun-soaked land where shadows creep,
A prickly friend dreams and refuses to sleep.
It's more than it seems, this bumpy old sage,
With a heart full of love, it's the wise ones' page.

When the lizards do dance, all tails in a whirl,
Our cactus dances too, with a prickly twirl.
It giggles at snakes, those slithery foes,
Waving its arms—like a funny, spiny show.

At dusk, it basks while the critters all gather,
Sharing their secrets, each joke makes them rather
Fond of the quirks of their hot desert home,
Where laughter's the lifeblood, and friendships can roam.

Lifeblood of the Golden Sands

Amidst golden grains, a tall figure stood,
Sipping on sunlight, as only it could.
The sands told stories with every soft breeze,
But the cactus just chuckled, "I'm here to tease!"

With blossoms so bright, it dressed to impress,
While ants marched along, no time for distress.
They carried their crumbs, tiny troops on a quest,
All while the cactus smirked, feeling so blessed.

On a warm summer's day, a shadow was cast,
As critters all gathered, their laughter amassed.
With every sharp joke, they shared in the fun,
The lifeblood of friendship beneath the hot sun.

A Landscape of Endurance

In the heart of this land, a cactus did stand,
With arms wide open, welcoming each band.
It taught all the critters to laugh through their strife,
For humor stays strong and can brighten your life.

Through sun and through storms, it swayed with delight,
While geckos and gophers danced through the night.
"Life may be prickly," it chuckled so wide,
"But smiles are the remedy, come take a ride!"

Beneath the grand stars, the friendships will bloom,
In this landscape of grit, where nothing feels gloom.
The tales will be spun, and they'll echo and cheer,
For laughter is mighty, and so very dear.

Stories of the Underdog

In a patch of dried-out land,
Lived a prickly plant, so grand,
Pals called it 'Spike', oh what a name,
With dreams of fortune and fame.

But every time it stood up tall,
A gust of wind would cause its fall,
Yet still it laughed, with roots held tight,
Determined to dance in the night.

Once came a bird, feathery and loud,
Mocked our Spikey friend in a crowd,
'You'll never grow, you're just a joke!'
But Spiky donned a charming cloak.

Said, 'Oh dear bird, your words are sweet,
But I've got grit, so take a seat!
With every poke, I'll find my way,
And shine through dark, another day.'

Sun-Kissed and Thorned

In the desert sun, a dance begun,
For a cactus with dreams, oh what fun!
It stretched its arms in a sunlit glow,
And jived to tunes only it could know.

With sunshine hugs and a thorny flair,
It boasted beauty beyond compare,
But oh, the bees, they buzzed around,
And left our plant feeling quite confound.

'What's the buzz?' it chirped with glee,
'Just a little poke, come sit with me!'
But bees were scared of that prickly dance,
So the cactus moved on, seeking romance!

Finally met a dandy bee,
Said, 'You're thorny, but I like your spree!'
Together they twirled, each spin and twist,
In the arid dance, no silliness missed.

Beyond the Searing Heat

In the land where the sun does bake,
A cactus stood, not one to break,
With a smile wide and colors bright,
It joked with shadows, oh what a sight!

'Seeking shade is for wimpy trees,
I thrive in heat, just try to tease!
Bring on the blaze, I'll soak it in,
For every drip, I'll wear a grin.'

A lizard strolled, in search of cool,
Said, 'You're a fool, to flaunt that rule!'
But the cactus winked, with spunky cheer,
'Hot's my game, so stick around here!'

With every joke and every pun,
It turned the heat into pure fun,
And as the sun set, deep and red,
The cactus smiled, 'Now time for bed!'

Resilient Roots

Beneath the dirt, where secrets sleep,
Live roots that giggle, dive, and creep,
They stretch so wide, they know no bounds,
Singing songs of joy, it's all profound!

'We're not just green, we're funny too!'
A root proclaimed, with sass in view,
'If you think we're plain, just take a peek,
We party hard, we've got technique!'

When storms rolled in, and skies turned gray,
The roots would laugh, 'Bring it our way!
We're built to bend, not break in fright,
We'll dance through mud, and shine so bright!'

'Every drop is like a drink,'
They joked while winking, with hearts in sync,
So here's a toast to roots so spry,
With every twist, they reach for the sky!

Sunburnt Stories of Survival

In the sun, they stretch so tall,
Telling tales of heat and fall.
With a laugh, I slather cream,
Dreaming dreams of shade, it seems.

Each time I roam this sandy land,
My neck's a shade of lobster planned.
With sunburnt pride, I greet the day,
While swatting flies that dance and play.

A lizard laughs, sunbathing too,
While I chase shadows, feeling blue.
The drinks are warm, the ice is gone,
But here we are, just me and dawn.

So I'll embrace the stubborn light,
With giggles shared, oh what a sight.
In this land where heat is king,
Every prickly poke makes my heart sing.

The Language of Prickles

In the desert, the cacti talk,
With prickly hugs and needle walk.
They share their woes in spiky prose,
While spurning shoes on dried-out toes.

A nod, a poke, a tender jab,
It's quite the friendship, a quirky fab.
With every laugh, a pinch they give,
Teaching me how to truly live.

Their blooms unfold a vibrant show,
Saying, "Come, join this prickly row."
And though they've got their bristly ways,
We laugh through life, through sunny days.

So if you find a spiky friend,
Embrace the pricks, it's worth the bend.
For in their world of twist and jest,
I've found a place where I am blessed.

Oasis of Solitude

Amidst the thorns, a treasure glows,
A tiny pond where laughter flows.
In solitude, I'm quite the sight,
Chatting with birds, from day to night.

But wait, a tumbleweed rolls by,
It laughs and twirls beneath the sky.
I sip my drink of sand and sun,
And chuckle at my lonely fun.

I'd trade my thirst for a good pun,
Or swap my hat for a needle gun.
Yet here I sit, with prickly peace,
In this lone spot, let worries cease.

So here's to quiet, to laughter grand,
In an oasis, a pricky land.
I raise a toast to all that's spiked,
For solitude can be quite liked.

Desert Dances: A Spiky Waltz

Underneath the blazing sun,
I wiggle, dance, and have some fun.
With each step, a prickly beat,
My cactus partners stomp their feet.

We twirl and sway, a dance so neat,
While keeping clear of fiery heat.
They stick around with points to share,
In silly moves, we kick the air.

A tumbleweed joins for good measure,
Bringing along its wobbly treasure.
With outstretched arms, we spin in glee,
A desert ball where all can see.

So grab a partner, join the spree,
In prickly waltz, just you and me.
For in this dance of sun and shade,
Together we'll never feel dismayed.

Sunswept Solitude

On a sunny day I stand quite still,
A lizard coiled beneath the grill.
I wear my hat, quite wide and bright,
While ants march on their daily flight.

The sun beams down, a golden thumb,
I'm sweating bullets, what a bummer!
The drinks are cold, the snacks look fine,
But all I want is some shade divine.

I wave to pals, they wave right back,
But then they tripped, oh what a crack!
Laughter echoes in the dry air,
As tumbleweeds tumble without a care.

In solitude, I ponder well,
The heat's a beast but laughs compel.
With every drip, I sing my tune,
A cactus diva under the moon.

Hues of the Hectic Heat

Colors clash in the blazing sun,
Sipping lemonade, oh what fun!
Bright yellow hat, pink shades I sport,
The heatwave's here, but I'll not abort.

Sweaty brows and wobbly chairs,
Friends cracking jokes, oh who cares?
It's a carnival of laughter and cheer,
In the day's embrace, we persevere.

Red as a chili, orange like juice,
The sun's a prankster, what a ruse!
We dance and shuffle, avoid the burn,
In shades so bright, we twist and turn.

As evening creeps with painted skies,
We gather 'round, beneath the guise.
The hues of heat, a vibrant shout,
With giggles shared, we laugh it out.

Sturdy Against the Storm

A gust of wind, oh, here it comes,
I brace myself, oh what fun!
The cactus wiggles in the gale,
While friends all shout, "Let's set sail!"

Rain drops fall like tiny blobs,
We dodge the puddles, we're not snobs.
Dressed in raincoats, patterned bright,
Each step we take feels like a fight.

Dancing 'round in muddy shoes,
Sliding down, we all just snooze.
The clouds can grumble, shout and roar,
But laughter echoes, who could ask for more?

Through stormy trials and the rain,
We leap and shout, we dance again.
The sturdy won't bend, we stand and cheer,
With joyous hearts, we'll persevere.

Nature's Armor

In the desert sun, I wear my best,
A coat of quirks, I jest and jest.
The prickles stand like tiny guards,
But underneath, I've got no scars.

I strut my stuff, so bold and free,
With nature's armor, can't you see?
A wobbly stance in shifting sand,
With giggles sprouting, oh so grand.

Poking fun at prickly plight,
While dancing shadows chase the light.
With each stumble, I find my ground,
In funny ways, sweet joy is found.

So toast to all, my prickly pals,
In every storm, we share our gales.
Our laughter shields, our love, it blooms,
In armor bright, we sweep the rooms.

Life Amongst the Stones

In a garden of rocks, I found a bright spree,
A jester among thorns, oh what glee!
With giggles and pokes, I'd waltz and I'd spring,
While the stones took a rest without a thing to bring.

The critters all chuckled, they laughed at my dance,
In the shade of a boulder, I'd take a chance.
A tumbleweed rolled by, with a wink and a grin,
Life here's a comedy — who needs to win?

The sun gives a nod, it likes my show,
While I stumble and trip in the bright overflow.
But every little prick, no cause for alarm,
These stones save my skin with their fortuitous charm.

So here's to the rocks, my delightful crew,
In a patch of the wild, where the oddities grew.
I treasure each moment, each quirk and each tone,
For laughter's the life when you're never alone.

Vibrance Against the Wind

Beneath a bright sky, a tussle unfolds,
Where colors are bold, and the laughter beholds.
The breeze gives a tickle, and petals take flight,
But I'm fending off gusts that act more like fright.

With a dance fit for jesters, I sway to my tune,
The boughs join the party, they shiver and swoon.
But oh, what a scene when the wind has its say,
And my fancy new hat flies whimsically away!

I chase after fronds, as they whirl in the air,
While giggling at weeds that pretend they're quite rare.
The sun gives a chuckle, it lights up the day,
In this garden of carnival where I love to play.

So here's to the whirlwind, the laughter, the spin,
With vibrance and whimsy, let the fun begin!
I dance through the clamor, a joy-filled pursuit,
In a world that's just singing, and I'm in a cute suit.

Prickly Promises

In a patch of the wild, where the spines make a pact,
A promise of sunshine, a laugh, and a tact.
With every sharp jab, my friends laugh and cheer,
Each poke brings a giggle, it's all crystal clear.

A tiny arachnid plays peek-a-boo shy,
As I trip on the ground, oh my, oh my!
They promise me treasures amid prickly delights,
But they're tangled in laughter, on these curious nights.

"Don't worry!" I chant, "for the fun's just begun,"
As I dodge and I weave in this shimmering sun.
With blossoms all chatting, they banter and tease,
Evoking a chuckle from the buzzing bees.

So here's to our promises, ridiculous and bold,
With petals of laughter, and stories retold.
For every sharp ouch, I'll wear like a crown,
In this garden of mirth, where no one's a frown.

The Serenity of Spines

Among the serene, where the tiny spines lean,
I chuckle at life and its whimsical sheen.
With every soft rustle, I hear stories unfold,
Of prickly adventures and treasures untold.

A ball of green sweetness with sass and some flair,
Is giving a lesson in how to beware.
But I toss and I tumble, it's all in good jest,
For amidst all the pokes, I've found myself blessed!

The sun winks a smile, as peppered clouds drift,
Each ray is a giddy, fun-loving gift.
With laughter like raindrops and smiles unforeseen,
This garden of spines is where I've been keen.

So here's to the fun, the jests as we sail,
With the serenest of spines, where joy will prevail.
For in every prick, my heart finds its song,
In this quirky patch of cheekiness, I belong.

Blooming Against the Odds

In a desert so dry, how do they grow?
With just a few drops and a hint of a glow.
They wiggle and giggle in sunshine so bright,
Flaunting their blooms in the broad daylight.

A party of spines gives the no-show a chance,
While they dance in the air like a green little dance.
Who knew such sharp things could be so carefree?
In a prickly old world, they just want to be.

Secrets Beneath the Surface

The sands hide tales that no one can see,
Like the secret lives of a cactus tree.
With roots that are tangled, they plot with a grin,
Life underneath is where the fun begins.

Whispers of laughter where shadows entwine,
A soggy old secret that's truly divine.
They gossip of rain in the middle of June,
And plan wild adventures by the light of the moon.

Mirage of a Distant Oasis

In the distance, a shimmer, a vision so rare,
The thirsty ones stumble, in fervent despair.
But alas! It's a trick that nature's conceived,
A mirage of joy, or so they believed.

"But look at me stretch, I'm a sight to behold!"
The cactus laughs softly, with spines oh so bold.
"Just close your eyes tight, let your dreams take a ride,
In this land of illusions, come join me outside!"

Shadows of Thorns and Dreams

In the twilight they gather, casting shadows of cheer,
Those prickly green giants, so whimsical here.
With dreams made of sunshine, they huddle so close,
Sharing tales of the winds and the plants they love most.

"Watch out for the bunnies that hop in the night,
They nibble our dreams, thinking it's a delight!"
Yet laughter erupts, for what's life without fun?
In the kingdom of prickles, their story's never done.

Guardians of the Parched Land

In a desert bright, they stand so bold,
Guarding secrets, stories untold.
With arms like spears and smiles so wide,
Nature's jesters, cactus pride.

When raindrops dance, they wear a crown,
Bouncing around in their spiky gown.
Wind whispers jokes, the sun will chuckle,
Life's a party in this prickly puzzle.

Creatures giggle, while shadows play,
Sipping moonlight, chasing the day.
Their thirst is vast, but appetite's great,
Dessert delight on a spiny plate.

Oh, look at them strut, what a sight to see,
Guardians of fun, from A to Z.
In the dry land, they play their role,
With humor and heart, they lift the soul.

Flourishing Amidst the Desolation

In barren lands, blooms pop up bright,
Cheering the gloom with a splash of light.
Their laughter echoes, a joyful burst,
Thriving in chaos, despite the thirst.

Each prickly hug, a fiesta chance,
Dancing in dust with a shaky stance.
Life finds a way, amid the dry,
Spiky revelers, oh me, oh my!

With laughter loud, like a party balloon,
Giggling with others under the moon.
Learning to thrive where few would dare,
Fashioning joy from the arid air.

Together they plot, tickling the sand,
Each thorny embrace, a helping hand.
In the desolation, they find their place,
Flourishing wildly in a spiky race.

Spines and Stars: Cosmic Connections

Under the stars, they share a laugh,
Starlit buddies in a spiky path.
Cosmic connect, with spines so grand,
Sharing tales of the desert land.

They whisper wishes to the wide dark sky,
Praying for rain, while birds just fly.
Each prickly pop a shoot to fame,
In the cosmic dance, it's all a game.

With starlight jokes and moonlit cheers,
Jesting away all their thirsty fears.
They plot their journeys with a wink so sly,
Among the comets, they reach to the sky.

Spines and stars, a humor-filled tale,
Traveling together, they'll surely prevail.
In the vast universe, they feel quite bold,
Creating laughter, a sight to behold.

Echoes in the Sand: A Green Saga

In the heart of dunes, a chime goes 'ping',
Echoes of laughter, what joy they bring.
A green saga unfolds in the heat,
Prickly pals dancing on tiny feet.

With echoes in sand, they craft their fate,
Guffawing wildly, oh isn't it great?
Life they proclaim in a wobbly spin,
Where the fun starts, let adventures begin.

Each day a circus, under the sun,
Throw in some spines, and you've got quite a fun.
Stories of survival, a binding thread,
In the warm, golden land, gales of laughter spread.

They jest with the shadows as day turns to night,
Echoes of mischief, a glorious sight.
In the sands of forever, they play their tune,
Cacti comedians, under the moon.

Resilience in Bloom

In a land where the sun does bake,
A prickly plant knows how to take.
With spikes like armor, bold and bright,
It laughs at drought, a humorous sight.

It sways in the wind with a casual flair,
Ignoring the heat, it doesn't care.
With stubborn roots that hold on tight,
A champion of 'endure and ignite'.

A friend to the lizard, oh what a pair,
Sharing secrets, a friendship rare.
In this dry kingdom, laughter blooms,
Against all odds, joy surely looms.

With each tiny flower, a burst of cheer,
Raising a toast to the dry frontier.
So here's to the spines, with wit and grace,
In a desert dance, they find their place.

Dry Elegance

In a coat of green, so sharp and fine,
Strutting around like it's divine.
With style unmatched, it takes a stand,
With quirky shapes all over the land.

The sun may try to rob its fun,
But look closer, watch it run.
With roots that giggle, ever sly,
It'll drink from puddles if they pass by.

Raindrops are gems in this sunburnt race,
Each drop a treasure, a source of grace.
With elegance found in spiky fashion,
Laughing delight is its true passion.

Its shadows stretch like a playful tease,
Waving to none but the desert breeze.
In a world of dry, it winks and chats,
A tale of class—all in spiky hats!

Desert's Hidden Wonders

Among the rocks, where few will tread,
Lies a quirky world, where laughter's fed.
With critters and blooms, each twist a surprise,
Hidden treasures, in the heat, they rise.

A footloose rabbit hops with glee,
While the wise old tortoise sips his tea.
Cacti wearing hats, oh what a sight,
Celebrating quirks under stars so bright.

The blooms break forth from spiny embrace,
Small bursts of joy in the parched space.
With each stubborn petal, a giggle erupts,
Nature's joke in the dry, it disrupts.

In the mirage of laughter, they thrive,
Playing hide and seek, how they strive!
These wonders remind, in the hot and the dry,
That joy can surface, if you only try.

A Dance of Shadows and Light

In the glow of dusk, the shadows play,
Sharp silhouettes join the ballet.
With a wink and a twist, the plants take flight,
In the desert air, they dance through the night.

Using their spikes as a funky guide,
They jive with the wind, full of pride.
Each twist of the spine, each tiny sprout,
Adding to laughter, there's never a doubt.

As the sun dips low, the colors bloom,
Creating a spectacle in the dusty room.
A cactus party, wild and free,
With shadows waltzing, as happy as can be.

So give a cheer for this desert show,
Where every prick brings joy, you know!
With a pep in their spines, they shine so bright,
In a dance of shadows and sheer delight!

An Oasis's Lament

In the desert sun, I wave my arms,
Calling for a breeze to soothe my charms.
But here I stand, a prickly joke,
Waiting for laughter—oh, what a poke!

The pools of joy are dry as bone,
My friends are rocks, or so I've grown.
I tell them puns, they just roll away,
I need a cactus friend to come and play!

A mirage of laughter floats in the air,
But when I reach, all I do is stare.
I'll keep my hope, it's quite the ride,
For humor blooms where others have dried!

So here's to jests, in the midday heat,
I'll plant a smile with every beat.
In the sand, I'll dance and sway,
An oasis of giggles, come what may!

Scripting Silence in Spines

I've got spines of wisdom jutting out wide,
With silent tales, a prickly pride.
Each thorn a story, but nobody reads,
I'm just a green statue planting my seeds!

At night, I ponder, a cactus bard,
My audience? Moonlight; that's not so hard!
I scribble jokes in the starry dust,
But they vanish at dawn—oh, how unjust!

I'd write a novel on how to stand tall,
But without a pun, it's a total fall.
In the desert, spines can't help but jest,
Even if silence feels like a test!

So here I wait, pen in hand,
Hoping to land a laugh—so grand!
With a poke, a jest, and a wink of light,
I'll bring some giggles to this endless night!

Flourish in the Drought

Amidst the sand with feet so bare,
I giggle at the sun with little care.
A drought might seem like a sad old tune,
But I thrive on laughter, morning to noon!

My roots dig deep in this arid sprawl,
While my humor rises, and echoes call.
I water my jokes with a sprinkle of glee,
And bloom with puns, just wait and see!

The cacti dance, we're quite the crew,
In the heatwave's grip, we find what's true.
A quip, a jest, we're never alone,
In this desolate land, joy is our throne!

So bring on the drought, we'll stand and twirl,
With roots in the ground, we'll show the world.
For laughter's the nectar we sip with glee,
In every dry moment, we flourish free!

Life in the Lonesome Land

In the lonesome land where shadows dance,
I crack a smile, it's my only chance.
The sun beats down and the sand winds sway,
My heart's a jester, come what may!

The bunnies hop, but I'm the one,
With endless jokes to fuel the fun.
I tell them tales of prickly dreams,
And they laugh so hard, no one hears my screams!

Here in the silence, my laughter rings,
Like rattlesnake songs and cactus flings.
In this lonesome lot, I'll find my tune,
Beneath the stars and the watchful moon!

So raise a glass of desert's delight,
To the humor found in the dark of night.
With spines and smiles in this sunburnt land,
I'll be the jester, just where I stand!

The Heartbeat of the Desert

In the sun on a hot, sandy day,
A spiky friend had much to say.
"I'm not a tree, don't give me shade!"
With a grin, the prickly prankster played.

Lizards dance on my prickly crown,
While squirrels giggle, running around.
"Is it a cactus or a dancing broom?"
In the vast desert, I bring the gloom!

With every poke, a laugh does spring,
My thorns like jokes that make birds sing.
Balloons would pop, yet I won't care,
Life's a party when I'll share!

In the warmth, I might look tough,
But playful pranks are never rough.
So join me in this sandy jest,
Let's tickle the desert, you'll love it best!

Tapestry of Thorns

In the desert, I weave a tale,
With prickly threads, I'll never fail.
A tapestry made of laughter's hay,
Stitching smiles in the sun's bright ray.

Thorns are fashion, they're all the rage,
My pointy style, like a desert sage.
"Try to hug me," the critters dare,
But it's all in fun, no need to scare!

Silly shadows dance on the sand,
A prickly court, oh, isn't it grand?
With laughter rolling like a tumbleweed,
In this tapestry, joy is our creed.

So join my thorns in this playful spree,
Together we'll weave a memory!
Because in this desert, laughter reigns,
With prickly friends, let's share our gains!

Sunlight and Shadows

In the sunlight, I stand so proud,
Casting shadows, a quirky cloud.
"Guess my shape!" the kids all shout,
As I wink and twist, dancing about.

With puffs of dust in a gentle breeze,
I wear the sun like a necklace, tease!
"What's the secret?" a lizard inquired,
"Just a little sun and all's required!"

Watch as I bend for a silly pose,
With shadows playing on friends' toes.
"Is it a plant or a funny hat?"
The desert giggles at the silly spat.

In this realm, where the sun is king,
Lighthearted moments make my heart sing.
So come, dear friends, under my shade,
We'll dance away, our woes will fade!

In the Dunes of Time

Time drifts like sand, with a chuckle or two,
In the desert's embrace, there's much to view.
With my prickly spires, I stand here bemused,
Watching the world, slightly confused!

Dunes play tricks, they hide and seek,
Every breeze gives a funny tweak.
"What did you say?" whispers the wind,
As I say, "Oh nothing, just a cactus grin!"

In my age, I've gathered some sass,
As tumbleweeds roll on, a humorous pass.
"Why so prickly?" the locals tease,
"Because my jokes are sharper than you, dear breeze!"

So here under stars, I'll tell my tales,
Of laughter and jest that never fails.
To the dunes of time, let's raise a cheer,
With prickly pals, life's always clear!

Prickly Tales Under the Sun

In the desert sun, a cactus sways,
Waving 'hello' in prickly ways.
It tickles the breeze in a funny dance,
While lizards do a double glance.

A roadrunner zooms, thinks it's all a game,
But the cactus just stays the same.
Chasing shadows, he runs real fast,
Yet the prickly friend just holds steadfast.

A party of ants makes their tiny trail,
Avoiding the spines, they're bound to fail.
One jumps high, lands smack on a thorn,
The cactus just laughs, "Oh dear, you're worn!"

With each little poke, a story is spun,
Of creatures and laughter in the blazing sun.
At sunset the spines tell tales so neat,
Of prickly friends making life sweet.

Silent Spines of the Desert

In the quiet night, oh what a sight,
Silent spines give the moon a fright.
A cholla dreams of a starry stew,
While saguaro hums a lullaby too.

The owls hoot, thinking they're sly,
But prickle edges are watching with eye.
"Who's having fun?" the night flowers bloom,
"Just us and the stars, in the desert's room!"

A tumbleweed rolls, with a giggle it skips,
Dodging the cacti and their sharp tips.
"Hurry up, friends, let's shimmy and sway,"
"Oh no!" says the cactus, "not my way!"

But laughter rings out beneath the soft moon,
With spines so sharp and hearts in tune.
For in this silence, with whispers and glee,
The desert thrives, wild and free.

Whispers of the Arid Night

In the stillness, a secret's told,
A cactus winks, it's feeling bold.
"Did you hear about the nightingale?"
"Sang to the spines, a funny tale!"

A family of javelinas trot by so spry,
With snouts of mischief, they give a sly sigh.
"Don't bump into me!" the prickly one pleads,
"The last time that happened, I grew more weeds!"

A shuffling tortoise, with shell shining bright,
Says, "I come in peace, it's all just light!"
The cactus chuckles, "Just take it slow,
With floral vibes we can steal the show."

As whispers float softly, laughter ignites,
In a land of spines where mirth takes flight.
With each little poke comes a giggle or two,
In the wilds of the night, a comical view.

Resilience in a Thorny Realm

In a world of thorns, the laughter grows,
With every poke, a story flows.
A sprightly bloom peeks out from afar,
"Life's a prickly journey, so raise the bar!"

The sun beats down; it's a dance of fun,
While critters scurry, all on the run.
A prickly pear party, oh what a sight,
With fruit hats on, they're feeling just right.

A horned lizard joins, with a dash of flair,
"Let's twirl and hop like we haven't a care!"
But a sharp little poke sends him back down,
He shakes off the water and brushes his crown.

In this thorny realm where laughter is king,
The resilience grows, and the joy bells ring.
From spiky beginnings, the friendships rise,
In this captivating land where humor flies.

Thorned Elegy of the Sun-Kissed Land

In a sun-soaked realm, life takes its stance,
A prickly affair, but oh, what a dance!
With needles like arrows, they sway with flair,
Laughing at wanderers, who dare to come near.

The flowers bloom bright, as they giggle and tease,
While shadows of giants play tricks in the breeze.
In each curve and point, a story they weave,
Of sunburnt mishaps that make you believe.

With water so scarce, they splash and they squirt,
Cracking the ground, you could call it a dirt concert!
The sun is their stage, the moon holds their light,
In this prickly kingdom, all life takes a bite.

So here's to the jests of this sun-kissed parade,
Where laughter blooms free, unbothered, delayed.
With each thorny hug, they spread joy and cheer,
In this wild, funny world, let's all gather near.

Echoes of the Elders: Prickly Wisdom

Listen, dear traveler, to tales of the wise,
With eyes full of laughter and sage-like surprise.
They babble of thistles and stolen gold light,
Witty and sharp, like a rogue in the night.

"Count not on the rain!" they cackle with glee,
"Survive on your wits, like you're sipping sweet tea!
Embrace every scratch, and wear it with pride,
For each little poke is a laugh we can ride."

Dance around cacti, they beckon and sway,
In their prickly embrace, we'll tumble and play.
The secrets they keep, hidden under their spins,
Are lessons in laughter, where the prickles begin.

So heed their strange wisdom, but take care, my friend,
In a land full of humor, let your journey extend.
For every sharp joke, is a poke from the heart,
In the land of the wise, we're never apart.

Carved by Time: A Tale of Survival

Out in the wild, where the tough stand tall,
Life's a rugged journey, but what's the call?
With arms wide open, the sturdy embrace,
Of a prickly façade, oh, what a space!

Each groove tells a story of sunburned delight,
Of storms that have danced through the perilous night.
With laughter embedded in every sharp twist,
They thrive through the chaos, they truly insist.

Through drought and through rain, their resilience sings,
Their antics are baffling, like juggling kings.
"Fear not the sharp thorns!" they jest and they boast,
"For survival is art, let's raise a glass toast!"

So sway with the winds, in wild, joyous plight,
In this dance of survival, hearts take flight.
Embrace every scar; they're badges of cheer,
In a world where we giggle, we conquer our fear.

Vibrant Silhouettes Under the Moon

As the silver glow wraps the desert at night,
The silhouettes wiggle, oh what a sight!
With laughter ignited by moonbeams so bright,
The prickly cast shadows, a jubilant rite.

Under a canopy of shimmering stars,
They mingle and jostle, just like rock guitars.
With each cheeky poke from the moon's gentle light,
The spines spin their tales, a whimsical flight.

They tell of the sun, the heat of the day,
While sharing sweet secrets, in a funny bouquet.
Behold the grand jesters of the silvery night,
In vibrant parade, they dance with delight.

So let's toast to the prickle, the bloom, and the jest,
In the tapestry woven where humor won't rest.
For life in the wild has its whimsy and charm,
In the shadows and light, find the laughter that warms.

Shadows Cast in Sand

In the desert, shadows dance,
Cacti laughing at chance,
With arms raised to the sun,
They've already had their fun.

A lizard weaves a tale,
Of prickly pears and ale,
While tumbleweeds spin round,
In a comedy profound.

Sand dunes begin to sway,
As the sun runs away,
With mirages playing tricks,
Like mischief from the sticks.

Yet every drop we find,
Is a treasure, never blind,
For in the heat's embrace,
We find laughter's warm face.

The Language of Aridity

In a land where voices shrink,
Cacti whisper, sip, and think,
They converse with the breeze,
In a language that aims to tease.

With thorns like quills, they write,
Messages of dry delight,
Each bloom a punchline bold,
In stories yet untold.

When rain clouds come to play,
The spines all shout, 'Hooray!'
But trickles turn to streams,
And wash away the dreams.

So here's to dry humor,
And secrets of the rumor,
Where laughter sprouts and grows,
In his desert, nobody knows.

Echoes of the Forgotten Oasis

Amidst the dunes so bare,
An oasis hides with flair,
Where cacti share a drink,
And all of life's a wink.

The date palms gossip loud,
To every wandering cloud,
With shadows stretching wide,
In the shade they all abide.

Rumors of water dance,
In each prickly romance,
As visitors arrive,
To sip and then survive.

Though forgotten, it's alive,
In this jolly, dry hive,
Where laughter echoes free,
In the stillness of glee.

Flora of the Forgotten

In this realm of dry and dust,
Lies a flora born of rust,
With ferns that sing off-key,
And flowers sipping tea.

A yucca with a grin,
Says, 'Who let the fun begin?'
While agaves in a trance,
Compete in a silly dance.

The blooms all share a joke,
With a tumbleweed bespoke,
While the sun begins to sway,
In this bright, absurd play.

So here's to nature's jest,
In spiny, prickly vest,
For in the heat we find,
A humor well-designed.

Oasis of Secrets

In the desert sun, the cacti sway,
With secrets to share at the end of the day.
They whisper and giggle, oh what a scene,
A prickly party, where fun's evergreen.

Their spines are their jokes, oh so dry,
Beneath the bright stars, they reach for the sky.
One cactus said, with a chuckle so bright,
"I'm just here for laughs, yeah, it feels just right!"

A lizard strolled by with a curious glance,
"Can I join the fun? Oh, give me a chance!"
They welcomed him close, for hilarity's sake,
In this quirky oasis, they'd giggle and quake.

So in the still night, with the moon up so high,
The plants threw a bash, oh my, oh my!
An ocotillo twirled, a yucca did prance,
Underneath the full moon, they all took a chance.

Tales of Arid Resilience

In a land where the sun shines hot as a fry,
Cacti tell tales with a wink in their eye.
They brag of the times they've weathered the drought,
"With a drink of the rain, we'll dance without doubt!"

A team of green folks, they stand tall and proud,
With stories of survival, they gather a crowd.
"Once I met rain, it was love at first sight!"
Said one spiky fellow, under stars shining bright.

They share all their quirks, with laughter and glee,
"Why did the desert get a cactus? Just me!"
They poke fun at the sun, with their laughter in sync,
Creating an oasis where humor won't sink.

So next time you stroll by their prickly abode,
Remember their stories, their laughs and their code.
Each spine hides a punchline, so sharp and so slick,
In this desert of laughter, the time ticks – so quick!

Thorned Tales of Survival

Out in the desert, where the tough plants thrive,
Lived a spiky bunch, just trying to survive.
Each thorn a reminder of battles they've won,
Their saga of strength is silly, but fun!

A tall saguaro said, with a twist of its trunk,
"I've had my fair share of life's playful funk!"
They chuckled and cringed at the tales of the past,
Of storms and adventures that left them aghast.

With a bounce in their stance and a giggle quite bold,
They told of a tumble that once left them cold.
"I fell on my side, what a terrible fate!"
But then they all laughed, 'It just wasn't our date!'

So in cactus circles, remember this truth,
Even tough little warriors can giggle with ruth.
Amidst all the thorns, there's resilience and play,
In the heart of the desert, they're funny all day!

Silent Stands and Stories

In the stillness of dusk, when the shadows grow long,
Cacti hold court, where the wise plant belong.
With spines full of tales and roots deep in jest,
They mingle and mix, far outdoing the rest.

"What do you call a dry plant on sand?"
One cactus inquired, its humor so grand.
"A cacti-mated joke, oh they grow by the ton!"
The laughter erupted, how they rolled in the sun.

Through the whispers of wind, their stories will soar,
Of friends who get stuck when they can't find the door.
"We've given up hope, but we're fine right here,
With thorns that hug tight, in the warmth, have no fear!"

So as they all chuckle at their prickly delight,
They dance in the moon—what a wonderful sight!
In the silence of stands, a symphony plays,
Of love, laughter, and joy—oh, what fun-filled days!

Shadows of the Desert Sky

In the night, shadows dance,
Cacti wear their prickly pants.
Lizards throw a wild soirée,
With desert moonlight in array.

Owls hoot like they own the place,
While jackrabbits pick up the pace.
Why did the cactus cross the land?
To get to the other sand.

A tumbleweed rolls and prances,
In this space, anything enhances.
The stars laugh, twinkling bright,
As desert critters take flight.

So raise a glass of prickly brew,
To the quirkiness that feels so true.
Under the sky, let's take our stand,
In this oddball, sandy wonderland.

The Sagebrush Serenade

In the sagebrush, tunes arise,
A chorus of coyotes and sighs.
Dancing in shadows, they perform,
While the tumbleweeds spin and swarm.

Gophers giggle, playing hide and seek,
In this dusty land, they're far from meek.
A cactus stood up, ready to sing,
Just waiting for the desert spring.

A rattlesnake plays the rattle drum,
While lizards dream of a tasty crumb.
The laughter echoes, wild and free,
In a quirky, prickly jubilee.

Who knew dry land could have such flair?
With every breeze, joy fills the air.
Here in the desert, we all agree,
Life is best when it's a spree!

Fragments of a Waterless World

In a world where water's a myth,
Cacti tell tales with a twist.
They sip on sunshine, oh so sly,
As clouds drift by and laugh on high.

A lizard prances, slick and spry,
Wondering how to touch the sky.
"Do you think I could catch a rain?"
He mused, "Or just dance with the pain?"

The sun plays games, a blazing star,
While critters gather from afar.
"Let's hydrate with thoughts," one quips,
"Or just enjoy our sunny trips."

Fragments of mirth flutter like leaves,
In a world where nothing deceives.
With cacti smiling, oh what a show,
In the land where laughter can grow.

Arid Elegies

In the heart of glare, where dry winds blow,
The cacti wear their hats, a dapper show.
An old sage whispers to the breeze,
"Embrace the heat; it's the desert's tease."

The lizards march in snapdragon lines,
While shadows stretch in playful designs.
"Who needs oceans?" they jest with glee,
"When sand is the dance floor for you and me!"

Underneath the vast, unyielding blue,
Dry tongues are dreaming of raindrops, too.
Yet laughter echoes in this dry space,
In arid elegies, we find our grace.

So gather close where the sunbeams play,
And let the quirky desert brighten our day.
In this land of thorns and hearty cheer,
We embrace the funny, year after year.

www.ingramcontent.com/pod-product-compliance
Lightning Source LLC
Chambersburg PA
CBHW070336120526
44590CB00017B/2911